To

Jang

Just a tad sick in places
but ever so funny :)

lau

Mags

Paul e Bump xx

D1639668

This Mother's Book is the property of the following mother:

....

....

Any children caught stealing this book
from their mum will be disowned
by Santa immediately.

At last, here is an antidote
to the cheesy schmaltz that
surrounds motherhood: a practical
guidebook that tells it like it is.

Packed with useful tools and tips,
it's what every contemporary
mother needs to make a success
of the mothering business.

With its help, you stand a
chance of ending up with fully
functional children. Without it,
you may as well hand them
over to Social Services.

Happy mothering!

PARENTAL LICENCE

This licence allows you to conceive and bring up children. It must be produced when required by Social Services, education authorities, the police, or other relevant government agencies.

IMPORTANT DOCUMENT! KEEP YOUR VALIDATED LICENCE IN A SAFE PLACE.

Name:	
Address:	
Date Of Birth:	
Signature:	

The above-named is licensed to mother an unlimited number of children.

Photo	Official use only
	SP ☐ PD ☐ Z ☐ Z+ ☐
	Fail ☐ Pass ☐
	Refer DHSS ☐ Refer DWP ☐
	Refer Inland Revenue ☐
	Refer NSPCC ☐ Refer RSPCA ☐

CHILDREN COVERED BY THIS LICENCE

Photo	Photo	Photo

Name:.................................
Date Of Birth:......................
Rank in order of preference:.........

Name:.................................
Date Of Birth:......................
Rank in order of preference:.........

Name:.................................
Date Of Birth:......................
Rank in order of preference:.........

Photo	Photo	Photo

Name:.................................
Date Of Birth:......................
Rank in order of preference:.........

Name:.................................
Date Of Birth:......................
Rank in order of preference:.........

Name:.................................
Date Of Birth:......................
Rank in order of preference:.........

PENALTY POINTS: Should you commit a parenting offence, you will incur penalty points on your licence. More than 12 points may lead to disqualification from parenting and your children being taken into care. The following is a non-comprehensive guide to the number of points that may be imposed. Forgetting your child's name: 2 points. Failing to change your child's nappy within current target time: 3 points. Parenting while alcohol level over the limit: 4 points. Raising your voice at your child: 5 points. Damaging your child's self-esteem: 7 points. Damaging your child's self-esteem permanently: 10 points. Beheading your child accidentally whilst messing around with knives and with alcohol level over the limit: 11 points.

Deciphering teenspeak: a glossary

Unnnnhhhh…
Hmmmmppff!
Huhunnnh?
Waaaaaaaaaahh??
I didn't ask to be born!
I hate you!!
It's so unfair!!!
Stop embarrassing me!!!!

Teenagers speak in a language all of their own, where every grunt is rich in meaning. Here are the basics:

That was a scrumptious meal, thank you!
You look lovely today, Mother.
I'll clean my room this instant.
I've done my homework, but I'll go over it once again, just to check.
I'm extremely grateful for the upbringing you're providing.
I love you and Daddy very much.
We may occasionally disagree, but I respect your parental authority.
You're the best Mum ever.

How to pick the perfect babysitter

Too pretty

Too young

Choosing a suitable babysitter is one of the most important mothering skills. To whom should you entrust your precious offspring? Who should you trust with the keys to your house? And last but not least, who should you trust not to run off with your weak-willed husband?

Too
weird
☒

Just
right!
☑

Compliments page

You won't get any direct appreciation from your cynical modern kids, so draw strength from the compliments on this page. Your children would say all these things if they could, but it's just not allowed under playground law.

"You're a good mother!"

"I really like the way you mother me!"

"Mum, you're doing great!"

"Mother, your parenting skills are nonpareil!"

Morning launch checklist

Every morning, run through the following checklist before releasing your children into the wild:

1. Pre-launch

2. Ears scrubbed

3. Nose wiped

4. Spots squeezed

5. Glasses cleaned

6. Teeth brushed

7. Hair combed

8. Attitude corrected

NB: The precise order of this checklist has been honed by thousands of mothers over centuries. Ignore it at your peril!

Womanly things to teach your daughter

Pass on that special feminine know-how gleaned over the years!

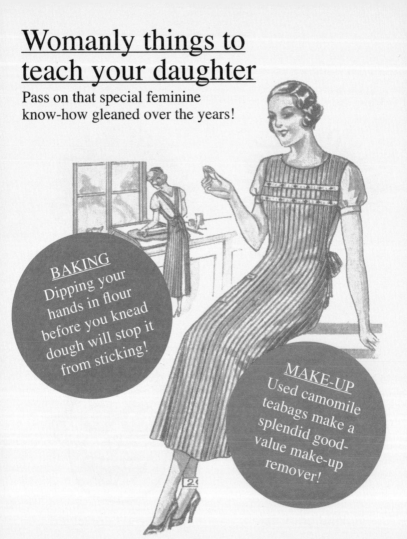

BAKING
Dipping your hands in flour before you knead dough will stop it from sticking!

MAKE-UP
Used camomile teabags make a splendid good-value make-up remover!

Baby talk

Babies are uniquely receptive. As you cuddle them, whisper useful advice in their ear, such as:

Lawyer is a great job, and so is doctor!

Teenage pregnancy is a big no-no!

Signs your teenager is doing drugs

Warning signal:
Teenager talks to you affectionately
Teenager performs all chores and homework in double time
Teenager's nostrils are superglued together
Teenager now has just one big nostril
Teenager is in jail in Thailand for 30 years
Teenager is slow to respond and spouts baffling nonsense

DANGER!

	Drug:
	Ecstasy
	Speedballs
	Glue
	Cocaine
	Heroin
	Marijuana*

* Or hormonal imbalance

How to make your kids love unpalatable vegetables

SPINACH:
"If you eat this, Mummy and Daddy will cancel divorce proceedings, we promise"

MUSHROOMS:
"They explode inside your stomach!"

BROCCOLI:
"Don't eat that, it's poisoned!"

RADISHES:
"Harry Potter can't get enough of these"

SPROUTS:
"They make you fart really noisily"

CAULIFLOWER:
"It's not a vegetable, it's a deadly invading alien"

CABBAGE:
"The cabbage company gives you a free TV for every hundred you eat"

CARROTS:
"Little Billy didn't eat his, and he died, in quite a lot of pain actually"

USEFUL NUMBERS

Children are always getting into trouble. Keep these on you at all times in case of emergency.

Emergency services	999
Missing Persons Helpline	0500 700 700
NHS direct	0845 46 47
Social Services	020 7712 2171
Sexual Health Line	0800 56 71 23
National Drugs Helpline	0800 77 66 00
Samaritans	0845 790 90 90
The Priory	01372 860 400
National Poisons Information Service	0870 600 6266
Hospital for Tropical Diseases	020 7387 4411
Floodline	0845 988 11 88
Air Accidents Investigation Branch	01252 512299
National Grid	01926 65 3000
Government Decontamination Service	0845 850 13 23
Legal Aid	0845 345 43 45
Crimestoppers	0800 55 51 11
AA (Automobile Association)	0845 788 77 66
AA (Alcoholics Anonymous)	0845 769 75 55
Gas Safety Helpline	0800 11 19 99
RSPCA	0870 555 59 99
UK Private Investigators	0845 257 32 74
Home Office	020 7035 4848
Serious Fraud Office	020 7239 7000
RNLI	0845 122 69 99
Anti-Terrorist Hotline	**0800 78 93 21**
London Stock Exchange	**020 7797 1000**
Ministry Of Defence	**020 7218 9000**
Foreign Office	**020 7008 1500**
Chinese Embassy	**020 7299 4049**
CNN News	**00-1-404-827-1500**
FBI	**00-1-202-324-3000**
White House	**00-1-202-456-1414**

Breastfeeding: Latest Techniques

Technique: **Old-school**
Psychological outcome:
Balanced personality,
if a little dull

Technique: **Whoops-a-daisy**
Psychological outcome:
Balanced personality, but
very prone to sea sickness

Technique: **Withholding**
Psychological outcome:
Insecure personality, with
trouble forming relationships

Technique: **Breast-switching**
Psychological outcome:
Attention deficit disorder /
manic personality

Breastfeeding can be a powerful formative psychological tool. Vary your technique to shape your child's personality, and help them stand out from the crowd when they grow up.

Technique: **Sharing with Daddy**
Psychological outcome:
Confused sexuality, with deep
ambivalence towards father figures

Technique: **Distance feeding**
Psychological outcome:
Good motor skills, lonely

Technique: **Left breast one
week, right breast the next**
Psychological outcome:
Schizophrenic tendencies

Technique: **Teen feeding**
Psychological outcome:
Severe confusion, though
very healthy bones

Spotting "dodgy" teachers

It's important not to be alarmist about this, but the tabloids don't lie: child abuse is rampant these days in our educational system. Here is how to spot the monsters in our midst.

1	Low eyelids (reptilian)
2	Slack jaw (from drooling)
3	Sweat (obviously)
4	Patterned jumper (distracts the children)
5	Unshaven bit (no woman in his life)
6	Glasses (all the better to prey)
7	Critical of your child's academic abilities (zero empathy)
8	Critical of your parenting skills (guilty as sin!)

Alert the *News of the World* on 0800 279 37 86

Car trips: Keeping the children busy

Most car games seem hopelessly old-school to the new generation of kids. Pick something with a more modern appeal, from the examples below:

ARE WE THERE YET?
"Every time anyone says this, tighten their seat belt by an extra inch."

NOW YOU SEE IT NOW YOU DON'T
"When the driving parent goes over the speed limit, put your hands over their eyes to punish them."

YANK IT!

"Test the solidity of the car's fixtures and report back to manufacturer for a refund."

I SPY!

"Spy fellow motorists whom you find ugly, and communicate this to them visually."

BALDIE!

"Giving each other haircuts makes for hours of fun."

DODGE IT!

"Throw empty crisp packets, drink cans and other objects out of the window at other drivers."

Monitor how proud you are of your children over the years

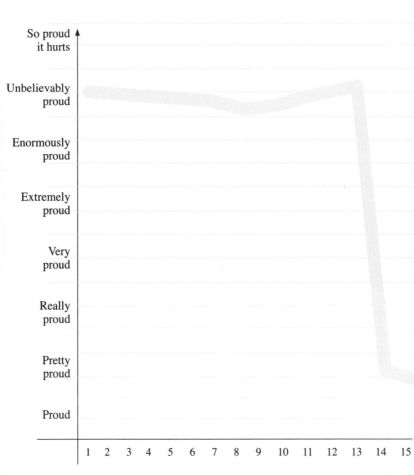

Pick one colour per child

....

....

....

....

....

Billy (example)

Age

16 17 18 19 20 21 22 23 24 25 26 27 28 29 30

Ageing well

Pinpoint which child is responsible
for each of your hairs going grey,
and deduct £1 from their inheritance.

Child responsible: Milo
Action: Burning down
nursery
Age: 3

Child responsible: Emily
Action: Microwaving
the gerbil
Age: 8

Child responsible: Tommy
Action: Hacking into Pentagon
Age: 12

Child responsible: Lizzie
Action: Going on the game to fund crack habit
Age: 17

Examples

This is a bar chart showing discipline methods.

No longer best practice (ordered left to right by height):

- Sending to orphanage
- Beating with red-hot poker
- Flogging
- Caning
- Spanking over knee
- Washing mouth with soap
- Shouting

Discipline:
Best practice

No TV

No dessert

Sending to bed early

Grounding for a week

Sending to "naughty space"

Therapy with counsellor

Prozac/Ritalin in cereal

Best practice

It's difficult to keep up with the latest trends in child discipline. One minute, a punishment is entirely socially acceptable; the next, it can land you in prison. Here is a guide to what constitutes current best practice.

Dealing with bullying

Pinch the bully's nipples with your nails and turn them 360°, whispering "I am Satan, child, fear me" into their left eyeball.

Open your handbag to reveal a kitchen knife that you will have dunked in calfs' brains beforehand. Dribble.

Bullying is a big social issue these days, and one that doesn't admit of easy answers. There is one way to deal with it, however: get the bully on their own, and do something so extreme to them that no one will believe it when they tell.

Use psychological warfare: "It's awfully kind of you to play with my child, even I don't dare touch him since the diagnosis."

Slowly lick the bully's face, casually saying "You taste nice, come round and I'll put you straight in the pot."

Choosing Godparents

These days, you cannot have too many. Make sure each child has at least:

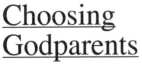

One rich godparent ☐
To provide for your child should you decease prematurely.

One foreign godparent ☐
To teach your child a marketable foreign language.

One nice
godparent ☐
To remember
birthdays even
if you don't.

One religious
godparent ☐
To teach your
child about God
(optional).

*Sacrifices
you have made
for your
children without
ever expecting
so much as a
thank you*

Career... ☐

Freedom... ☐

Sleep... ☐

Time for yourself.............................. ☐

Dreams.. ☐

Independence................................... ☐

Privacy.. ☐

Waistline... ☐

Travel to exotic places..................... ☐

Meetings with exotic people............. ☐

Affairs with exotic strangers............ ☐

Best years of life............................. ☐

Was it worth it? Yes ☐ *No* ☐

Would a thank you help? Yes ☐ *No* ☐

Too late now ☐

<u>Leaving the nest</u>
There comes a day when your precious darlings can no longer hide under your wing and must fly off to face the big wide world on their own. This is not a cause for sadness, but for tears of joy. Bid them farewell and wish them every success in life.

What if they refuse to leave the damn nest?
These days, kids end up living at home into their thirties and forties if you let them. Here are a few effective ways of kicking them out:

1. Make the nest less comfortable.
Turn the heating down. Get rid of the TV. Stock only macrobiotic food. Turn their 5-star hotel into a hovel that even a hermit wouldn't put up with.

2. Make the nest hell.
Having their parents walk around naked all the time is pretty much a child's version of hell. Remember to turn the heating back up, though.

3. Vacate the nest.
Rent your home out to a poor family with ten kids, and go on a cruise for a few months. When you return, your child will have left. Now evict the family.

4. Destroy the nest.
As a last resort, you may have to scupper the nest. Arson will do the trick, though try not to take the neighbours down with you.

The "Cosmic Reward Chart"™

DAY 1	DAY 2	DAY 3	DAY 4	DAY 5
DAY 6	DAY 7	DAY 8	DAY 9	DAY 10
DAY 11	DAY 12	DAY 13	DAY 14	DAY 15
DAY 16	DAY 17	DAY 18	DAY 19	DAY 20
DAY 21	DAY 22	DAY 23	DAY 24	DAY 25
DAY 26	DAY 27	DAY 28	DAY 29	DAY 30

Make your own chart and stickers out of cardboard or empty cereal boxes!
simply order the ... from ... ...itewillchangeyourlife.com for £29.99 a month.

This simple reward wallchart will not only help motivate your children, but will also educate them about our galaxy in the process. Place one sticker on the chart every day, reflecting your child's behaviour.

Stickers

	SPACESHIP: When your child does something good, like tidy their room, they get a spaceship.
	STAR: Once their good behaviour has earned them ten spaceships, they can use them to reach a star.
	BLACK HOLE: When they do something bad, they lose a spaceship; if it's very bad, such as soiling themselves, they lose a star.
	ALIEN: It's important to learn that life is fickle. Occasionally remove all the rewards they have earned so far, and start again from scratch.
	GALAXY: Once they have accumulated fifty stars, they rule the galaxy! Reward them with a biscuit or other suitable prize.

TOPICS TO DISCUSS WITH PEOPLE OTHER THAN HOW UNIQUELY GREAT YOUR CHILDREN ARE

Keep at hand in social situations and consult
whenever people's eyes start to glaze over

The weather	What's on TV
Haute cuisine	Bill Gates
Renaissance art	Prescription drugs
Ming ceramics	GM crops
Football	New Hollywood film
Holidays	Hobbies
Climate change	Pollution (bad)
The death penalty	Crime (rising)
The government	Morals (declining)
Immigration	Public transport (issues with)
Taxes	Beaujolais Nouveau
Visits to the doctor	Tabloid headlines
Brands of pet food	The death of the high street
Shopping	Medical complaints
Shoes	Latest fad
Consumer electronics	Celebrities (new)
The latest pope	Celebrities (old)
Spam email	Existential vacuum of life
Sexual trends	Problems in Africa
Smoking	Abortion
Drinking	Death
Brahms	Ebola
Geopolitics	The weather

Bedtime Stories

Help your little darlings fall asleep promptly by warning them about the monsters that will come if they don't.

The one who sucks your liver out through your nostrils:

The one who stitches your mouth up so you can never eat ice cream again:

The one that strips your skin off and wears it as his pyjamas:

The one who squeezes your nipples
until you run out of screams:

The one who kisses you to death
with his great spiky tongue:

The one that makes you eat all your own
snot until you're so fat you explode:

The one that tickles your toes until you
can't bear it and chop them off yourself:

Sleep tight!

MOTHE

Every mother who owns this book is eligible to participate in Mother Idol, Benrik's new reality TV show to find the world's best mum!

CRYING GAME
Contestants are handed a crying baby each: who will shut it up first?

SCHOOL-GATE BATTLE
The mother who talks up her kids most convincingly wins!

FOOD FIGHT
Cook for the UK's fussiest kids. The mum with the cleanest plate triumphs!

ER IDOL

TEMPER TEST
Keep your cool as your children break your most treasured possessions – live!

SPEED NAPPY
How many nappies can you change per minute?

TEEN TALK
Mothers have to joust verbally with the world's lippiest teens!

SPECIAL PRIZE!
Winner gets to adopt a Malawian orphan!

To apply, visit www.thiswebsitewillchangeyourlife.com

Of all the maternal drives, the drive
to nurse one's young through illness
is probably the deepest and most
poignant. But how do you know if
your young are just trying to con you
into letting them off school?
Here is how to assess the merit
of some common symptoms:

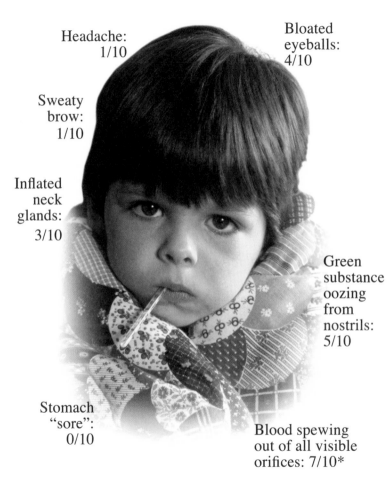

Headache:
1/10

Bloated
eyeballs:
4/10

Sweaty
brow:
1/10

Inflated
neck
glands:
3/10

Green
substance
oozing
from
nostrils:
5/10

Stomach
"sore":
0/10

Blood spewing
out of all visible
orifices: 7/10*

Don't say:

"I'll show you how he likes his Y-fronts ironed; he's very fussy."	"If I were her age again, young man, I'd definitely fancy you too!"
"What are your long-term intentions regarding my daughter?"	"If you get bored of her, there's always her younger sister."
"Aren't you a bit ugly for her?"	"Don't bother cooking her dinner, she'll only throw it up later."

Motherhood Test
How good a mother are you?

How would you describe your children?
Little angels!...+5
Little devils!...+4
Little shits!..+1

How do your children describe you?
The best mum ever!...+6
A lovely, yummy mummy!..+4
Don't know, the child psychiatrist wouldn't tell....+2

Were your children conceived:
After careful deliberation and planning................+5
As "happy accidents"...+5
Too drunk at the time to remember......................+1

Your offspring obviously come from a superior species. Here is a guide to spotting some of the more common differences between them and lesser breeds.

Geek — Insolent

Deformed — Badly brought-up

Unclean — Born loser!

Not your child

Comparing your children to others

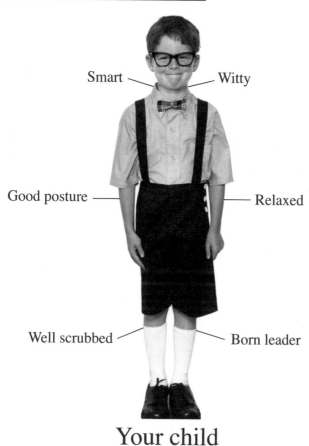

Smart

Witty

Good posture

Relaxed

Well scrubbed

Born leader

Your child

Teen rebellion

The best way to thwart teenage anger is to rebel yourself. Your teens will naturally react against you and lead impeccably upright lives.

1. Wear revealing mini-skirts.

child's beloved

Do say:

"I do hope you use condoms, he had a nasty wart when he was eleven."

"Would you like a cup of tea, dear?"

"Aren't you too pretty for him?"

"I guess you're an improvement on the last floozie."

If you liked The Mother's Book, you'll love The Father's Book!

Features:
- Top 10 excuses for forgetting a child's birthday
- Dancing in front of your children: the rules
- Choosing your child's career for them
- Facts of life: telling it straight
- Good riddance: marrying off your children
- Helping with homework: the cheat sheet
- Post-natal abortion: your rights

How much quality time do you spend with your kids?

At least 25 hours a week.......................................+4

10–25 hours...+3

1 hour (maximum visiting time).............................+2

In your old age, do you expect your children will:

Take you into their home to live as one big happy family...+9

Take proper care of you no matter the expense....+5

Take sweet revenge..+1

Results

Over 25 points: You're so perfect you make all the other mothers look useless. Well done!

Between 15 and 25 points: You're a pretty good Mum, certainly the best your kids will ever have.

Under 15 points: This book comes too late to help. See if you can get your money back.